Developing Numeracy
HANDLING DATA

ACTIVITIES FOR THE DAILY MATHS LESSON

year
3

Hilary Koll and Steve Mills

A & C BLACK

Contents

Reprinted 2004, 2005
Published 2002 by A & C Black Publishers Limited
37 Soho Square, London W1D 3QZ
www.acblack.com

ISBN 0-7136-6297-2

Copyright text © Hilary Koll and Steve Mills, 2002
Copyright illustrations © Michael Evans, 2002
Copyright cover illustration © Charlotte Hard, 2002
Editors: Lynne Williamson and Marie Lister

The authors and publishers would like to thank Jane McNeill and Corinne McCrum for their advice in producing this series of books.

A CIP catalogue record for this book is available from the British Library.

Printed in Great Britain by St Edmundsbury Press Ltd, Bury St Edmunds, Suffolk.

A & C Black uses paper produced with elemental chlorine-free pulp, harvested from managed sustainable forests.

Introduction

Developing Numeracy: Handling Data is a series of four photocopiable activity books for Key Stage 2, designed to be used during the daily maths lesson. It focuses on the fifth strand of the National Numeracy Strategy *Framework for teaching mathematics*. The activities are intended to be used in the time allocated to pupil activities; they aim to reinforce the knowledge and develop the facts, skills and understanding explored during the main part of the lesson. They provide practice and consolidation of the objectives contained in the framework document.

Year 3 supports the teaching of mathematics by providing a series of activities which develop essential skills in collecting, representing and interpreting numerical data. On the whole the activities are designed for children to work on independently, although this is not always possible and occasionally some children may need support.

Year 3 encourages children to:
- solve a given problem by organising and interpreting numerical data in
  - Venn and Carroll diagrams
  - simple lists and frequency tables
  - pictograms (symbol representing one or two units)
  - bar charts (intervals labelled in ones or twos);
- interpret and respond to questions about given data;
- plan, collect, represent and analyse data in a variety of forms.

Extension

Many of the activity sheets end with a challenge (**Now try this!**) which reinforces and extends the children's learning, and provides the teacher with the opportunity for assessment. The instructions are clearly presented so that children can work independently. On occasion, you may wish to read out the instructions and explain the activity before children begin working on it. For some of the challenges, the children will need to record their answers on a separate piece of paper. Sometimes the activity will require children to represent data in the form of a graph or chart and squared paper (or alternatively a computer with a handling data package) may be necessary.

Differentiated activities

Some of the activity sheets within this book are differentiated. A less challenging activity is indicated by a rocket icon: and a more challenging activity is indicated by a shooting star icon: . These activity sheets could be given to different groups within the class, or all children could complete the first sheet and children requiring further extension could then be given the second sheet.

Organisation

Very little equipment is needed, but it will be useful to have available: rulers, sharp pencils, squared paper, scissors, coloured pencils, counters, dice and ICT handling data software packages. You will need to provide a UK atlas for page 8 and coins for page 34. A blank bar chart, and blank Venn and Carroll diagrams are provided on pages 44 to 46.

The activities in this book could be incorporated into lessons for other curriculum subjects, for example history, ICT, geography or science. The National Numeracy Strategy recommends exploiting opportunities for drawing mathematical experience within other primary subjects, and handling data is a topic rich in cross-curricula investigations.

To help teachers select appropriate learning experiences for the children, the activities are grouped into sections within this book. However, the activities do not have to be used in that order unless otherwise stated. The sheets are intended to support, rather than direct, the teacher's planning.

Some activities can be made easier or more challenging by masking or substituting some of the numbers. You may wish to re-use some pages by copying them onto card and laminating them; some others you might want to enlarge onto A3 paper.

ICT

On most occasions where pupils are asked to represent data in a graphical or tabular form, a computer could be used for this purpose. Some programs allow more than one type of graph to be drawn, and comparisons of this type are very useful. Spreadsheets could be used to assist children in collecting information or as part of a survey.

Where children are researching their own topics for handling data, safe Internet sites could be used. Acceptable sites can often be accessed through a local educational authority's website or through kid-safe searches as part of most search engines. Some websites are suggested on page 5 and in the teachers' notes.

Teachers' notes

Brief notes are provided at the foot of each page giving ideas and suggestions for maximising the effectiveness of the activity sheets. These can be masked before copying.

Whole-class warm-up activities

The following activities provide some practical ideas which can be used to introduce or reinforce the main teaching part of the lesson, or to provide an interesting basis for discussion.

Pictograms and bar charts

Counting in steps

Practise counting in steps of two before doing activities that involve pictograms where a symbol represents two units or bar charts with a scale labelled in twos. Arrange children in a ring and count round so that each child says a number. Count forwards from zero to 50 and backwards again to zero. Say two even numbers and ask the children to give the odd number that lies between the two. Then say an odd number and ask the children to say the two even numbers either side of it.

Pick a pictogram

You will need some circles of the same size (you could use sticky paper circles). Cut some of the circles in half to make semicircles. Give each child a circle or a semicircle. Explain that each semicircle is worth one unit. Choose several children and ask them to stand and hold up their shapes. Ask: *How many is this worth? How many is one circle worth?* Begin by choosing two or three children, then gradually increase this to include more. Group pairs of semicircles together to make whole circles, representing two units. This activity can be adapted so that each semicircle represents two, five or even ten units.

Venn and Carroll diagrams

Magic Kingdom

This game helps children to recognise familiar properties of numbers. Tell them that certain numbers are allowed into the Magic Kingdom, while others are not. Give numbers in pairs, where one has the property and the other has not, for example: *The number 15 is in the Magic Kingdom, but 7 is not. The number 20 is in the Magic Kingdom, but 12 is not.* Encourage the children to work out what the Magic Kingdom numbers have in common and to guess the rule. Once children think they know the rule, they should give a pair of new numbers in the same way rather than telling everyone else what it is.

Serious sorting

Draw a Venn or Carroll diagram, like those on pages 45 and 46. Begin to write numbers on the diagram and invite children to guess the rule for each section, for example, write even numbers into one ring and numbers less than ten into the other, with even numbers less than ten in the intersection. Once children have guessed the rules, they should come up and write new numbers in the correct sections of the diagram rather than telling everyone else the rules. Continue until all the children have discovered the rules, then label the diagram.

Easily accessible sources and further ideas

The following suggestions for real-life data can be used as a stimulus for further data work.

Newspapers These contain a wealth of information, for example: TV programme listings, football tables, sports results, temperature readings and weather reports. They can also be analysed with questions such as *How many letter As are in this report?*

Travel brochures Children can investigate temperatures, compare prices, find out which destinations have most hotels with swimming pools, and so on.

Magazines Look for survey results presented in charts or graphs for the children to interpret, as well as questionnaires that the children can answer themselves.

The school and children themselves Investigate measurements of objects in school, different ball diameters, growth of houseplants/seedlings, children's standing jump results, cooking and food technology activities, activities children undertake at home and so on.

Calendars Children can analyse the information on calendars. Ask questions such as: *What day is the first/last/sixth of each month? In which month do most children in the class have a birthday?*

Useful websites
www.standards.dfes.gov.uk/numeracy
www.dinosaurworld.com/facts.html
www.metoffice.gov.uk/education/data
www.schoolhistory.co.uk
www.georesources.co.uk

Greedy gorilla

- **Look carefully at the picture.**

- **Count each type of fruit. Fill in the table.**

Fruit	Number
bananas	6
pineapples	
pears	
apples	
bunches of grapes	
melons	

1. Of which fruit are there the most? _____

2. Of which fruit are there the fewest? _____

3. Of which fruit are there exactly three? _____

4. How many pieces of fruit are there in total? _____

There were ten of each fruit to start with.

- **Which is the gorilla's favourite fruit?** _____
- **How do you know?** _____

Teachers' note Encourage the children to count carefully, possibly marking each fruit as it is counted. Ensure that they check the total number of pieces of fruit in two ways, for example, by totalling the numbers in the table and by counting all the fruit in the picture. Ask further questions such as: *Of which fruit are there two more than the number of pears? Of which two fruits are there the same number?*

**Developing Numeracy
Handling Data Year 3
© A & C Black**

Cups of coffee

- **Do you think** [most] **teachers in your school drink more than four cups of coffee each day?**

  yes ☐   no ☐

- **Use this table to help you check your guess.**

This will be an approximate number.

Names of teachers	Number of cups each day

- **How many teachers drink:**

  more than four cups? _____

  four cups or fewer? _____

- **Was your guess right?** _____

- **Now draw a** [bar chart] **to show the information in your table.**

Number of teachers

Number of cups

Teachers' note This data could be collected prior to the lesson – a child or pair could be sent to each teacher. If your school has a large number of teachers, ask the children to survey a small section of the teachers, for example those in Year 3. Ensure the children realise that the numbers given are likely to be estimates only. For the extension, the children could use the blank bar chart on page 44.

Developing Numeracy Handling Data Year 3 © A & C Black

- **Look at the map. It shows some cities in the United Kingdom.**

Most cities in the United Kingdom have more than seven letters in their name.

No they don't!

Sam

Ali

Aberdeen

Edinburgh

York

Manchester

Norwich

Belfast

Liverpool

Birmingham

Cardiff

London

Exeter

Canterbury

- **Who do you think is right?**

Sam	Ali	Can't tell
☐	☐	☐

- **Now write the number of letters for each city.**

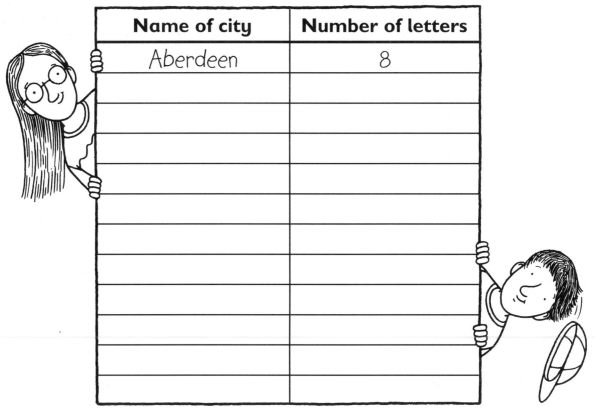

Name of city	Number of letters
Aberdeen	8

- **Is this information enough to say whether Sam is right? Look at a UK atlas to help you decide.**

Teachers' note Show the children city names in a UK atlas and encourage them to test Sam's hypothesis more fully. As an extension, the children could sort the names into three sets, for example, those with 5 letters or fewer, those with 6 to 8 letters and those with more than 8 letters.

**Developing Numeracy
Handling Data Year 3
© A & C Black**

Train-spotting

At a busy station there are engines with ⌐1⌐ carriage, ⌐2⌐ carriages, ⌐3⌐ carriages and ⌐4⌐ carriages.

- **Draw a table like this to show the information.**

Engines with 1 carriage	
Engines with 2 carriages	
Engines with 3 carriages	
Engines with 4 carriages	

1. How many engines have:

(a) exactly 1 carriage? _____   **(b)** exactly 3 carriages? _____

(c) fewer than 3 carriages? _____   **(d)** more than 3 carriages? _____

2. Which is the most common number of carriages? _____

3. Which is the least common number of carriages? _____

Now try this! The engines with ⌐3⌐ carriages leave the station.
- **How many engines are in the station now?** _____

Teachers' note Encourage the children to draw their table on squared paper. They could tick each engine as it is counted. Ensure that they use their table to answer the questions. As a further extension, the children could work out the total number of carriages before and after the engines with three carriages leave the station.

Developing Numeracy
Handling Data Year 3
© A & C Black

9

Jack's week

- **Read the note. It shows the jobs Jack did to help around the house during one week.**

On Monday and Thursday I did the washing up.
On Friday and Wednesday I laid the table.
On Monday, Saturday and Sunday I walked the dog.
On Saturday I unpacked the shopping.
On Sunday I washed the car and I also tidied my room.

- **Complete the table.**

Day of the week	Number of jobs
Monday	2
Tuesday	
Wednesday	
Thursday	
Friday	
Saturday	
Sunday	

Jack's mum gave him 10p for each job he did.

- **Complete this** pictogram **.** (10p) **stands for each job.**

Monday	(10p) (10p)
Tuesday	
Wednesday	
Thursday	
Friday	
Saturday	
Sunday	

Now try this!

- **How much money did Jack earn in total?** _____

Teachers' note Some children may be able to use tallying to complete the table. Ask further questions that involve interpreting the table and the pictogram, for example: *How many jobs did Jack do on Thursday? On which day did he earn the most money? How much did he earn at the weekend? How much did he earn during the week?*

**Developing Numeracy
Handling Data Year 3
© A & C Black**

Computer games

The pictogram shows how many games Lara played on her computer during one week.

Monday	🖥️ 🖥️
Tuesday	🖥️ 🖥️ 🖥️
Wednesday	
Thursday	🖥️
Friday	
Saturday	🖥️ 🖥️ 🖥️ 🖥️
Sunday	🖥️ 🖥️ 🖥️ 🖥️ 🖥️ 🖥️ 🖥️

🖥️ stands for ＿＿ game

1. How many games did Lara play on Tuesday? ＿＿＿

2. How many games did she play on Friday? ＿＿＿

3. On which day did Lara play only two games? ＿＿＿＿＿＿＿

4. On which day did she play four games? ＿＿＿＿＿＿＿

5. On which day did she play the most games? ＿＿＿＿＿＿＿

6. How many games did Lara play during:

   (a) Monday to Friday? ＿＿＿ **(b)** Saturday and Sunday? ＿＿＿

7. Why do you think she played more games at the weekend?

   ＿＿＿＿＿＿＿＿＿＿＿＿＿＿＿＿＿＿＿＿＿＿＿＿＿＿＿

8. Lara goes to ballet two nights a week. Which two nights

   might they be? ＿＿＿＿＿＿＿＿＿＿ and ＿＿＿＿＿＿＿＿＿＿

9. Lara plays an extra game on Sunday.

   Draw this on the pictogram.

 • **How many games did Lara play in the whole week? ＿＿＿**

Teachers' note This sheet can be used where the computer symbol represents one unit or two units. Before photocopying, write either '1' or '2' in the blank to create the appropriate key (making 'game' plural if '2' is inserted). If the symbol represents two units, discuss how one game would be represented, i.e. using a picture of half a computer.

**Developing Numeracy
Handling Data Year 3
© A & C Black**

Favourite toy: 1

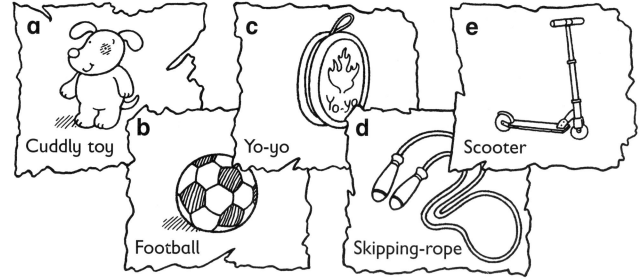

a Cuddly toy
b Football
c Yo-yo
d Skipping-rope
e Scooter

- **Which of these toys do you like best?** _____

- **What letter is this toy?** _____

- **Find out which toy each child in your class likes best.**

Child's name	Letter	Child's name	Letter	Child's name	Letter

- **Now draw a pictogram like this to show how many children chose each toy.**

  Use **to stand for two children.**

  Use (to stand for one child.

Cuddly toy	☺ ☺
Football	☺ ☺ ☺ (
Yo-yo	
Skipping-rope	
Scooter	

Teachers' note Before photocopying, write the names of the children in your class into the table. With the whole class, call out the names in turn. Ask each child to say their favourite toy, while all the children write this letter down. Some children may find it easier to draw a pictogram where one face represents one child. The following sheet provides questions relating to the pictogram.

Developing Numeracy Handling Data Year 3 © A & C Black

Favourite toy: 2

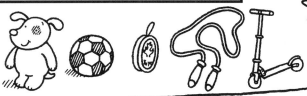

• **Use your pictogram to answer the questions.**

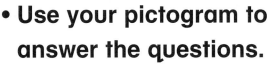

Which was the most popular toy? _____	Which was the least popular toy? _____
How many people chose the yo-yo? _____	How many people chose the skipping-rope? _____
How many people chose the cuddly toy? _____	How many people voted altogether? _____
Which was more popular, the yo-yo or the scooter? _____ How many more chose it? _____	Which was more popular, the football or the cuddly toy? _____ How many more chose it? _____
Did any two toys get the same number of votes? _____	Which toy do you think would be the most expensive to buy? _____
What is the difference between the number who chose the yo-yo and the number who chose the skipping-rope? _____	What is the difference between the number who chose the football and the number who chose the scooter? _____
Did more than one half of the class choose the same toy? If yes, which toy was it? _____	Was there a toy that fewer than five people chose? If yes, which toy was it? _____

Teachers' note The children should first have completed the activity on page 12. They should answer the questions in relation to the pictogram they drew in that activity. Further questions can be asked about the specific numbers of children choosing each toy, for example: *Which toy was chosen 11 times? Which toy was voted for six more times than the skipping-rope?*

**Developing Numeracy
Handling Data Year 3
© A & C Black**

A cross teacher

Class 3M made this pictogram. It shows how often their teacher got cross at school each day last week!

Monday	☹
Tuesday	☹
Wednesday	
Thursday	☹ ☹
Friday	☹ ☹ ☹ ☹
Saturday	
Sunday	

☹ stands for the teacher getting cross twice

1. How many times did the teacher get cross on:

(a) Sunday? _____   **(b)** Friday? _____

(c) Wednesday? _____   **(d)** Tuesday? _____

2. On which day did the teacher get cross:

(a) three times? _____   **(b)** twice? _____

3. (a) On which days, other than Wednesday, did the teacher **not** get cross? _____

(b) Why do you think that was? _____

_____

Now try this!

Monday	1
Tuesday	4
Wednesday	3
Thursday	0
Friday	2
Saturday	6
Sunday	7

This shows the number of times Ellie's mum got cross in a week.
- **Draw a pictogram of this.**
- **Make up questions about your pictogram for a partner to answer.**

Teachers' note It is important when children are interpreting graphs and charts that they are asked to use their own initiative rather than just finding the information straight from the chart, for example, by being asked questions such as *Why do you think that...?* or *Do you think this will always happen?*

**Developing Numeracy
Handling Data Year 3
© A & C Black**

Eye, eye?

A class made a pictogram of the colour of their eyes.

Blue	
Green	
Brown	
Grey	

> 👁 stands for 2 children

1. Which is the most common eye colour? _____

2. Which is the least common eye colour? _____

3. How many children have:

(a) blue eyes? _____   **(b)** grey eyes? _____

(c) green eyes? _____   **(d)** brown eyes? _____

4. How many more children have green eyes than grey? _____

5. How many more children have blue eyes than green? _____

6. How many more children have brown eyes than blue? _____

7. (a) Do you think brown is always the most common

eye colour? _____

(b) How could you find out more information about this?

_____

Now try this!

Two more children arrive in the class.
One has blue eyes and one has grey eyes.
• **Draw this on the pictogram.**

Teachers' note Encourage the children to find out more information about eye colour, surveying children in the class or school, adults in their homes, and so on. Ensure the children realise that just because something is true for a small group, it does not necessarily hold true for everyone.

Developing Numeracy
Handling Data Year 3
© A & C Black

What's hatching?

These pictograms show how many eggs were laid each day in three weeks.

• **Match each statement to the correct pictogram.**

◯ stands for 2 eggs

Week 1

Monday	◯◯◯
Tuesday	◯◯◯◯◖
Wednesday	◯◯
Thursday	◯◯◯◯◖
Friday	◯◯◯
Saturday	◯◯◯
Sunday	◯◖

Week 2

Monday	◯◯
Tuesday	◯◯◯◖
Wednesday	◯
Thursday	◯◯◯◯◖
Friday	◯◯◯
Saturday	◯◯◯◖
Sunday	◯◖

Week 3

Monday	◯◯◯◯◯◯
Tuesday	◯◯◯◯◖
Wednesday	◯◯◖
Thursday	◯◯◯◖
Friday	◯◯◯◯
Saturday	◯◯◯◖
Sunday	◯◯

Four eggs were laid on Wednesday.

Six eggs were laid on Friday.

Seven eggs were laid on Tuesday.

The same number of eggs was laid on Tuesday as Saturday.

The same number of eggs was laid on Tuesday as Thursday.

Two more eggs were laid on Friday than on Thursday.

Two more eggs were laid on Thursday than on Saturday.

Fewest eggs were laid this week.

Now try this!

• **True or false? During the three weeks there were:**

never fewer than two eggs each day _____

always more than 30 eggs each week _____

Teachers' note The children could explore the total numbers of eggs laid each week, find the smallest and largest daily number of eggs, work out whether there are more days when the number of eggs is 7 or more or when there are fewer than 7, find the most common daily number, and so on. The information could also be represented in a table.

Developing Numeracy Handling Data Year 3 © A & C Black

This is a game for up to six players.

You need one copy of the gameboard on page 18 and a dice.

You each need this sheet and a different-coloured counter.

☆ Each player chooses a flavour from the list along the bottom of the bar chart. Write the players' initials below the flavours.

☆ Place your counters on the **start** square of the gameboard.

☆ Take turns to roll the dice and move in any direction. The aim is to buy an ice cream from each van. You can only go to each van once.

☆ When you reach a van, you buy your flavour of ice cream. Everyone colours this on their bar chart.

☆ The winner is the first player to buy seven ice creams.

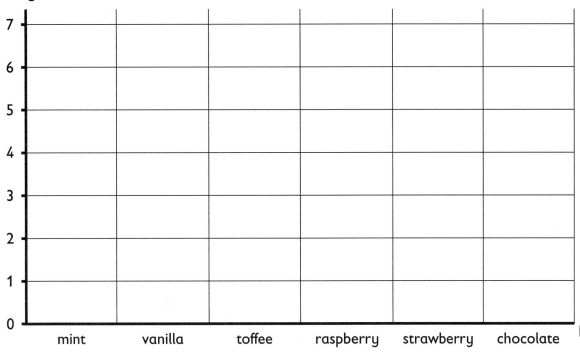

Number of ice creams bought

7
6
5
4
3
2
1
0

mint   vanilla   toffee   raspberry   strawberry   chocolate   **Flavours**

_____   _____   _____   _____   _____   _____

Teachers' note This sheet should be used in conjunction with the gameboard on page 18. The bar chart scale could be altered to show 0, 2, 4, 6, 8, 10, 12, 14. In this case the children should visit each van twice and the winner would be the first child to buy 14 ice creams.

**Developing Numeracy
Handling Data Year 3
© A & C Black**

I scream for ice cream: 2

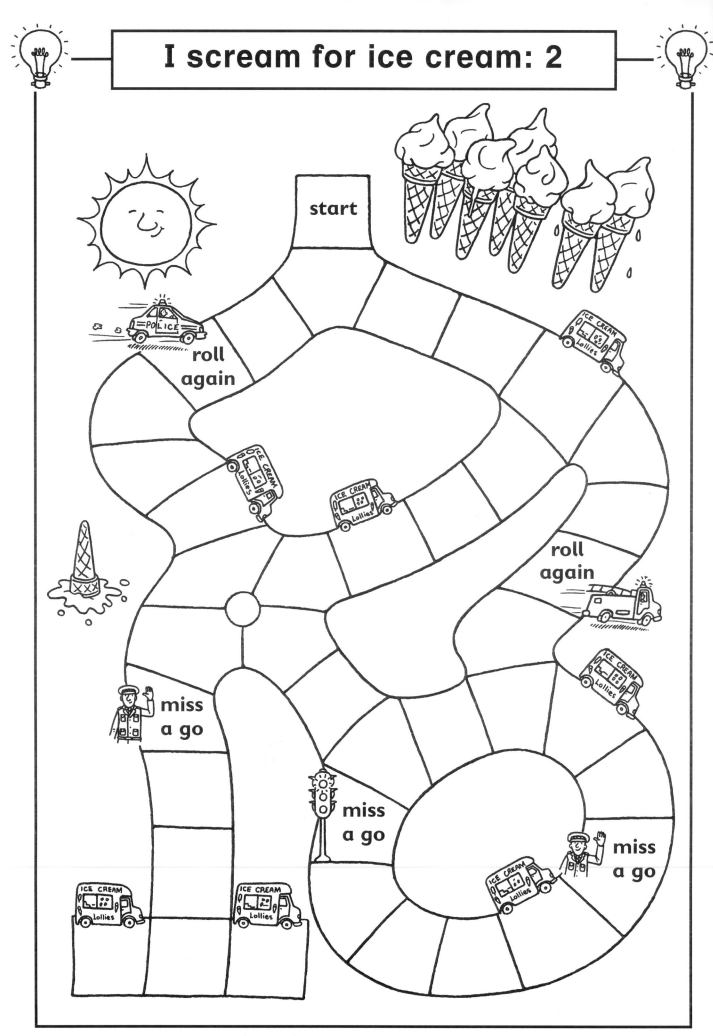

start

roll again

roll again

miss a go

miss a go

miss a go

ICE CREAM Lollies

Teachers' note This sheet should be used with the activity on page 17. Only one copy of this is required per group of up to six players. If possible, photocopy the sheet onto A3.

Developing Numeracy Handling Data Year 3 © A & C Black

Ladybird, ladybird...

- **Cut out the cards.**
- **Which ladybirds have the same number of spots? Sort them into groups.**
- **Draw a bar chart to show this.**

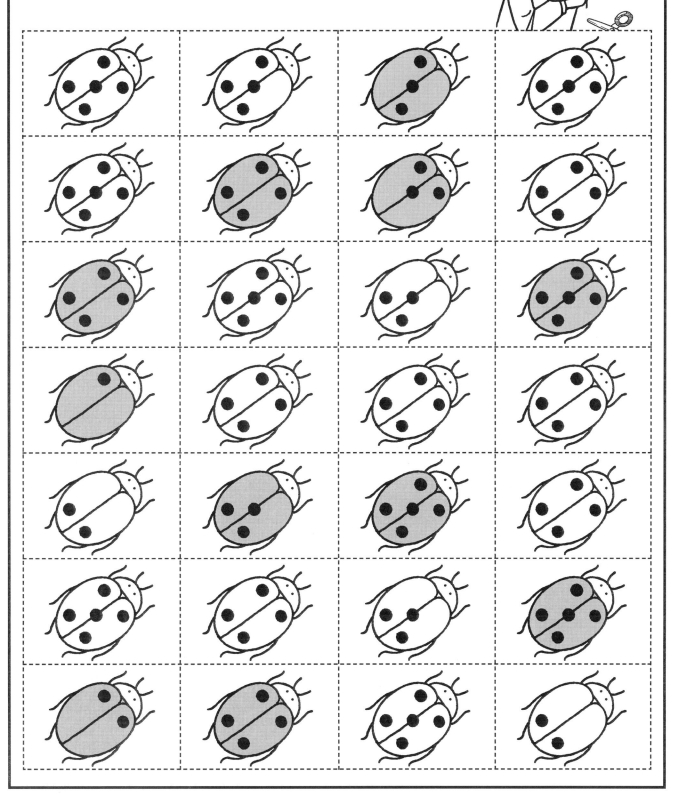

Teachers' note The blank bar chart on page 44 could be used with this activity. Tell the children to mark the horizontal scale 'Number of spots' and the vertical scale 'Number of ladybirds'. The children could write statements or make up questions about their bar charts. These cards can also be sorted onto Venn diagrams using the two intersecting criteria 'More than 3 spots' and 'White ladybirds'.

**Developing Numeracy
Handling Data Year 3
© A & C Black**

Spooky party

• **Count each type of spook. Complete the bar chart.**

Number
of spooks

**A bar chart to show the number
of different spooks at a party**

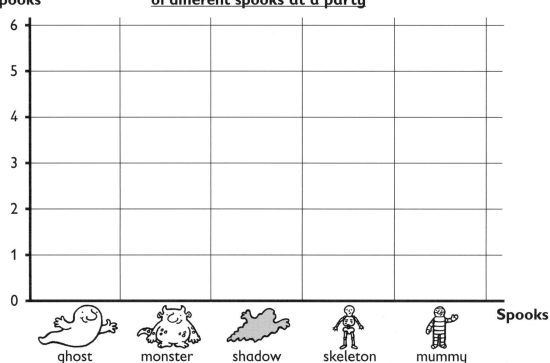

6

5

4

3

2

1

0

ghost   monster   shadow   skeleton   mummy

Spooks

1. How many: **(a)** skeletons? _____   **(b)** ghosts? _____

   (c) mummies? _____   **(d)** monsters? _____   **(e)** shadows? _____

2. Are there more mummies than skeletons? _____

3. Are there more shadows than monsters? _____

4. How many more ghosts than skeletons? _____

 • **How many spooks are there altogether?** _____

Teachers' note Encourage the children to count carefully, possibly marking each spook as it is counted. They could record their counting in a frequency table. Ensure that the children check the totals in two ways, for example, by totalling the numbers of all the bars on the chart and by counting all the spooks in the picture. The children could write statements about the information in the chart.

**Developing Numeracy
Handling Data Year 3
© A & C Black**

How many bikes?

- **Here is our class list. Find out how many bikes there are at each child's home.**

Child's name	Number of bikes	Child's name	Number of bikes	Child's name	Number of bikes

- **Now draw a bar chart like this to show the information.**

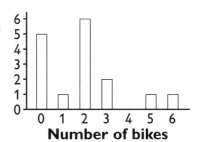

- **Use your chart to answer the questions.**

1. How many homes have:

    (a) no bikes? _____ **(b)** three bikes? _____ **(c)** four bikes? _____

2. Which is the most common number of bikes? _____

3. What is the largest number of bikes in one home? _____

4. How many children took part in the survey? _____

- **Now find out how many cars there are at each child's home.**
- **Draw a bar chart to show the information.**
- **Compare this with the number of bikes.**

Teachers' note Before photocopying, write the names of the children in your class into the table. With the whole class, call out the names in turn. Ask each child to say the number of bikes in their household, while all the children write this number down. They could draw a frequency table to help organise the information. Ask the children to write five statements about the information in their bar charts.

**Developing Numeracy
Handling Data Year 3
© A & C Black**

Creature feature

- **How many of each creature can you see in the picture? Draw a bar chart to show the information.**

- **Write five statements about the data in your bar chart.**

Teachers' note The blank bar chart on page 44 could be used for this activity. The intervals could be labelled in ones or twos. The children could also draw a frequency table to help them record their data. Once the bar charts are completed, ask: *How many rabbits are there? How many more cows than butterflies are there? What is the total number of creatures in the picture? How many are flying?*

Developing Numeracy Handling Data Year 3 © A & C Black

Who's not here?

• **Look carefully at this bar chart.**

A bar chart to show the number of children in Class A away from school in one week

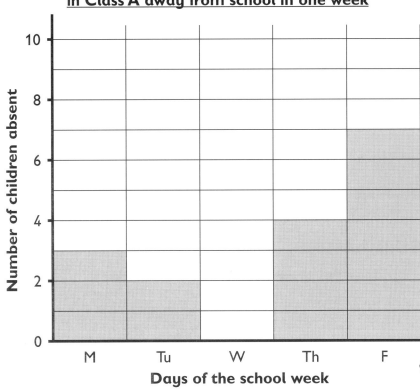

Number of children absent

Days of the school week

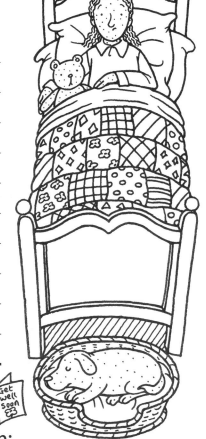

Get well soon

1. How many children in total were away on:

   (a) Tuesday and Thursday? _____ **(b)** Friday and Monday? _____

2. How many more were away on Friday than Tuesday? _____

3. How many more were away on Thursday than Monday? _____

4. On which days were there **fewer than** three children away?

   _____

5. If there were 34 children in total in Class A, how many children were at school on:

   (a) Monday? _____ **(b)** Friday? _____ **(c)** Tuesday? _____

Now try this!

• **Find out how many children in your class were away each day last week.**
• **Draw a bar chart to show this information.**

Teachers' note Some children may need to have the bar chart labelled in ones. Spend time discussing the bar chart before the children tackle the questions. Ask the children to use their own ideas to interpret the data, for example, by considering on which day children in Class A might have started to come down with flu. For the extension, the blank bar chart on page 44 could be used.

Developing Numeracy Handling Data Year 3 © A & C Black

Money box: 1

- **Look at the bar chart. It shows the number of different coins in Chloe's money box.**

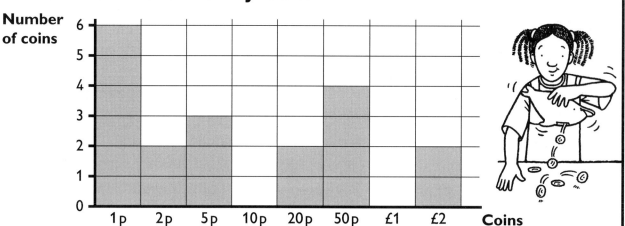

- **Draw the four missing coins.**

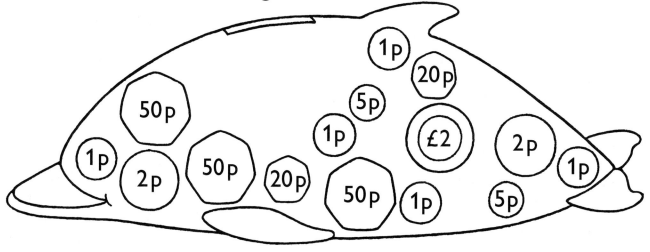

Chloe spends £2.76. She pays with exactly five coins.

- **Complete this bar chart to show the coins left in her money box.**

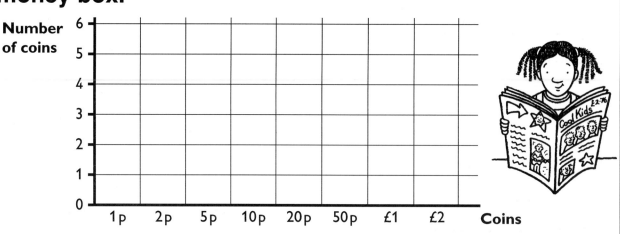

Teachers' note As an extension, the children could be asked to draw a bar chart to show the number of coins in Chloe's money box if she then paid for something costing £1.13 with a £2 coin. The activity on page 25 provides questions which require interpretation of the first bar chart.

Developing Numeracy
Handling Data Year 3
© A & C Black

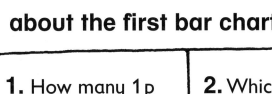

You need the sheet called Money box: 1.

- **Follow the trail. Answer the questions about the first bar chart.**

1. How many 1p coins does Chloe have? _____

2. Which coin does she have exactly three of? _____

3. How many silver coins does she have? _____

5. How many round coins does she have? _____

4. She has exactly two of three different coins. Which coins are they?
_____ _____ _____

6. How many coins does she have that are worth more than £1? _____

7. How many coins does she have that are worth more than 10p? _____

8. How many coins does she have that are worth less than 10p? _____

9. How many coins does she have altogether? _____

10. What is the total value of the 5p and 1p coins? _____

12. How much more money does she need to buy something costing £7? _____

11. How much money does she have altogether? _____

Teachers' note To complete this sheet the children will need a copy of the first bar chart on page 24. Some children may benefit from using coins to help them answer the questions. Use question 3 as an opportunity to discuss the fact that a £2 coin is both silver and bronze.

**Developing Numeracy
Handling Data Year 3
© A & C Black**

Triffic traffic: 1

- **Look at the number of people in each car.**

- **Fill in the table.**

Number of people in each car	Number of cars
1	
2	
3	
4	
5	

- **Now complete the sheet called Triffic traffic: 2.**

Teachers' note Use this with the activity on page 27. Encourage the children to count carefully, possibly marking each car as it is counted. Ensure that they check the total number of cars in two ways, for example, by totalling the numbers in the table and by counting all the cars in the picture. Use this context to explore whether the cars in this traffic jam are being used efficiently.

**Developing Numeracy
Handling Data Year 3
© A & C Black**

26

Triffic traffic: 2

You need the sheet called Triffic traffic: 1.

• Use it to complete this bar chart.

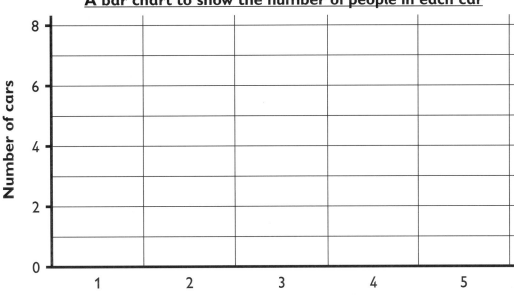

A bar chart to show the number of people in each car

Number of cars (vertical axis: 0, 2, 4, 6, 8)

Number of people in each car (horizontal axis: 1, 2, 3, 4, 5)

1. How many cars held:

(a) three people? **(b)** four people?

(c) five people? **(d)** one person?

(e) at least four people?

(f) fewer than three people?

2. Four cars held the same number of people. How many

people were in each car?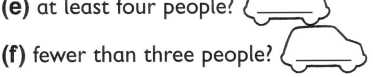

3. How many cars were there altogether?

4. One quarter of the cars held the same number of people.

How many people were in each car?

5. How many people were in the traffic jam altogether?

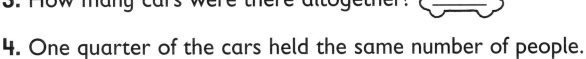

Teachers' note Use this with the activity on page 26. Note that the bar chart has a vertical scale marked in units of two. Some children may need to label it in ones. Further questions can be asked, for example: *Twice as many cars held three people as how many people? Do you think most cars on the roads contain three people? How could we find out?*

**Developing Numeracy
Handling Data Year 3
© A & C Black**

- **Look around your classroom. Write how many:**

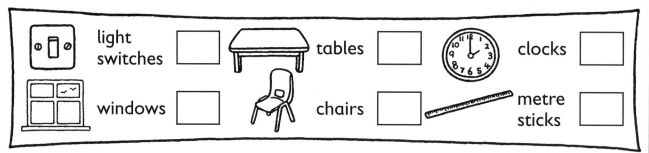

light switches ☐   tables ☐   clocks ☐

windows ☐   chairs ☐   metre sticks ☐

- **Now record this information on the bar chart.**

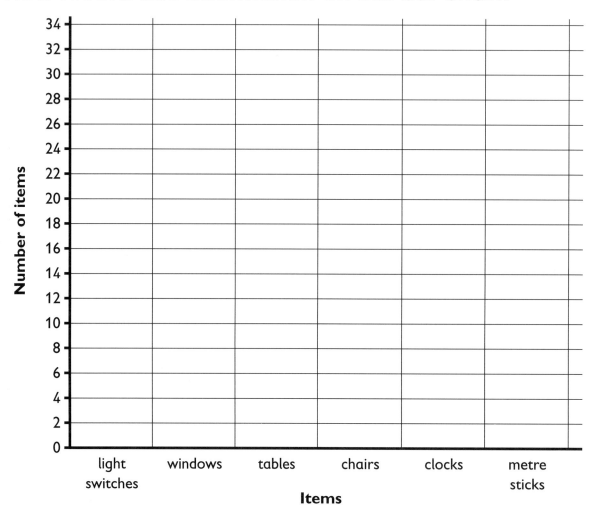

Number of items (y-axis: 0, 2, 4, 6, 8, 10, 12, 14, 16, 18, 20, 22, 24, 26, 28, 30, 32, 34)

Items (x-axis: light switches, windows, tables, chairs, clocks, metre sticks)

Now try this!

- **Write five statements about the data in your bar chart.**
- **Do you think most classrooms in your school have similar numbers of the items?**

How could you find out?

Teachers' note Check that the number of these items in your classroom is 34 or fewer. If greater than 34, the children could draw the chart on a computer or squared paper. Encourage them to discuss the data, for example, by comparing the number of chairs with children, and the number of chairs with tables. Give the children the opportunity to survey different classrooms and compare the data.

**Developing Numeracy
Handling Data Year 3
© A & C Black**

During the Second World War, each person in Britain was only allowed to buy a certain amount of food each week. The food was measured in ounces.
This bar chart shows how many ounces of different types of food a person was allowed.

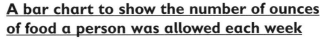

A bar chart to show the number of ounces of food a person was allowed each week

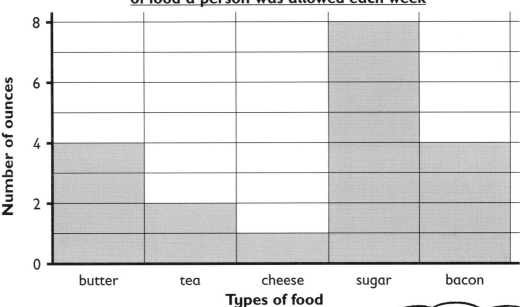

Number of ounces

Types of food

butter | tea | cheese | sugar | bacon

Each person was also allowed 1 egg, 3 pints of milk and 8p worth of meat. Other foods like rice, jam, biscuits, tinned fruit and dried fruit were rationed by points.

Each person had to register with one shop and this was the only place they could buy anything. Every person in a family had a ration book, even children and babies.

Teachers' note Ensure that the children understand the idea of rationing. Use practical equipment to help them appreciate the mass of one ounce (approx. 28 grams). Discuss this information sheet with the children before giving them one of the activities on pages 30 and 31. The children could research these ideas further using books or websites such as www.schoolhistory.co.uk.

**Developing Numeracy
Handling Data Year 3
© A & C Black**

Rations

• **Look carefully at the Rations information sheet.**

1. How many ounces of these was a person allowed each week?

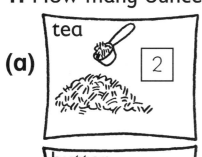

(a) tea 2

(b) bacon ☐

(c) butter ☐

(d) sugar ☐

2. How many ounces of cheese could one person buy in:

(a) one week? _____   **(b)** three weeks? _____

3. Each week, how many eggs was each person allowed? _____

4. If there were six people in a family, how many eggs could the family buy each week? _____

5. How many pints of milk could one person buy in:

(a) one week? _____   **(b)** three weeks? _____

6. Which could a person buy more of – butter or sugar? _____

7. How many more ounces of butter than tea could a person buy? _____

Teachers' note The children will need a copy of page 29 for this activity. Children requiring more challenging questions can be given the sheet on page 31. It is a good idea to have correct masses of the items available for the children to handle, to help them appreciate the ration quantities.

Developing Numeracy
Handling Data Year 3
© A & C Black

Rations

• **Look carefully at the Rations information sheet.**

1. How many ounces of these was a **family of four** allowed each week?

(a) tea ☐ 8

(b) bacon ☐

(c) butter ☐

(d) sugar ☐

2. How many ounces of cheese could one person buy in **five** weeks? _____

3. How many ounces of sugar could one person buy in **five** weeks? _____

4. Each week, how many more ounces of sugar than cheese could a person buy? _____

5. A person could buy the same number of ounces of butter as which other type of food? _____

6. Each week, how many pints of milk could a **family of four** buy? _____

7. Mrs Jones lived on her own. If she needed 24 ounces of sugar to make some jam, how many weeks would she have to wait? _____

Teachers' note The children will need a copy of page 29 for this activity. Children requiring less challenging questions can be given the sheet on page 30. It is a good idea to have correct masses of the items available for the children to handle, to help them appreciate the ration quantities.

**Developing Numeracy
Handling Data Year 3
© A & C Black**

Number sort

• **Look at the numbers in the ring. What do they have in common?** _____

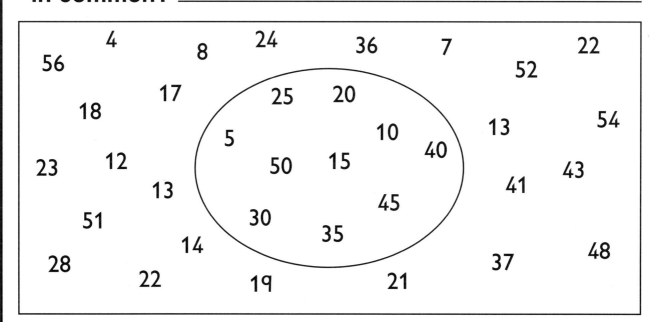

• **Sort the numbers 1 to 20 onto this** Venn diagram **.**
Numbers that do not belong in the ring go outside it.

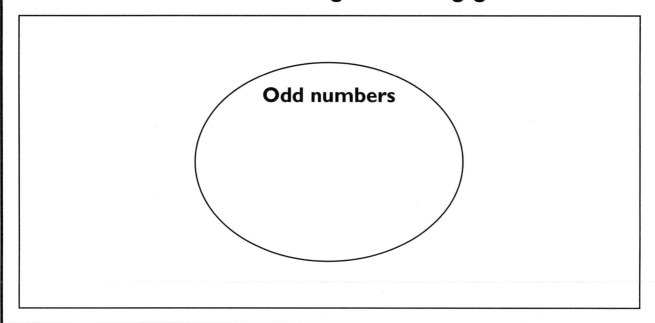

Odd numbers

• **Draw a similar diagram.**
• **Label the ring** Less than 10 **.**
• **Sort the numbers 1 to 20 onto it.**

Less than 10

Teachers' note This sheet can be used as a lead-in to the activities on page 33 and then page 35. This allows children to be guided slowly from one-criterion diagrams to two-criteria intersecting diagrams. For the extension activity, the blank Venn diagram at the top of page 45 could be used.

**Developing Numeracy
Handling Data Year 3**
© A & C Black

A machine sorts chocolate boxes into sets, according to the number of chocolates in each box.

Numbers that do not belong in either ring go outside them.

• Sort these chocolate boxes.

13 33 14 27 19 21 22 32 24 18 23

31 39 34 28 29 17 26 25 35 16

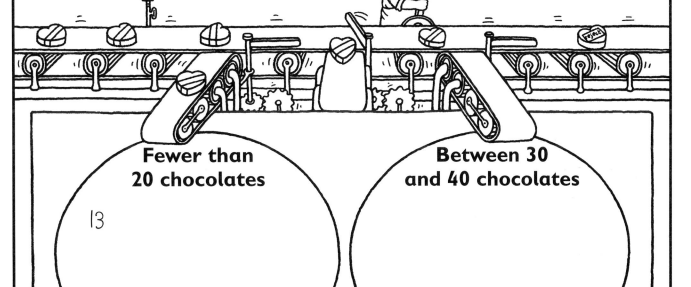

Fewer than 20 chocolates

13

Between 30 and 40 chocolates

1. How many boxes have fewer than 20 chocolates? _____

2. How many boxes have between 30 and 40 chocolates? _____

3. How many boxes are in neither ring? _____

4. How many boxes are there altogether? _____

• **Write three more numbers in each ring.**

Teachers' note This sheet can be used as a lead-in to intersecting Venn diagrams (see page 35). Discuss with the children how, if the criteria were altered, intersecting rings would be necessary. The criteria could be masked to provide a flexible resource. Other criteria such as 'More than 20 chocolates' and '20 chocolates or fewer' could be used (use criteria that are mutually exclusive).

**Developing Numeracy
Handling Data Year 3
© A & C Black**

Round and silver

• Play this game with a partner.

☆ Place the correct coins on the pictures.

☆ Take turns to roll the dice and move your counter in any direction.

☆ Take the coin you land on, if you can. Place it on the correct part of the Venn diagram.

☆ Keep playing until all the coins are on the diagram.

You need:
• a Venn diagram labelled 'Round' and 'Silver'
• two counters
• coins   • a dice

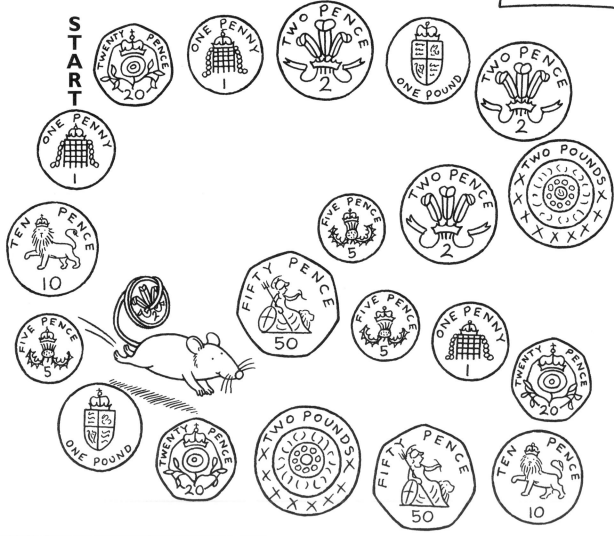

START

• Make up a new coin to go in the outside area of your Venn diagram. Draw and colour it.

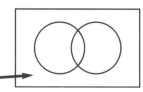

Teachers' note Provide each pair of children with an enlarged copy of the intersecting Venn diagram on page 45. Ask them to write the criteria 'Round' and 'Silver' on it, or do this yourself before photocopying. Discuss the intersection, if necessary, and the colour of the £2 coin. A similar activity could be done using the criteria 'Worth more than 10p' and 'Silver'.

Developing Numeracy Handling Data Year 3
© A & C Black

Multiple madness

- **Sort these numbers onto the Venn diagram.**

~~14~~ ~~7~~ 10   3   2   5   12   16   9   17   30   6   15   18   11

8   21   22   24   25   13   19   28   29   20   27   23   1   4   26

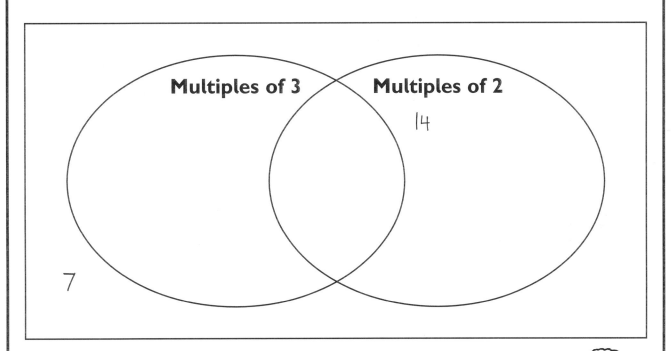

Multiples of 3   Multiples of 2

14

7

- **Look at your Venn diagram.**

1. How many numbers are multiples of 3? _____

2. How many numbers are multiples of 2? _____

3. **(a)** List the numbers that are multiples of both 3 and 2.

_____

   (b) Which other number are these multiples of? _____

4. Which numbers are not multiples of 3 or 2?

_____

5. Write two more numbers in each part of the Venn diagram.

Now try this!

- **Draw a similar diagram. Label the rings**
  Numbers greater than 15 **and** Even numbers .
- **Sort the numbers 1 to 30 onto the diagram.**

Teachers' note Ensure that the children know the meaning of the word 'multiple'. The top part of the sheet could be used again by masking and altering the criteria. The two criteria must *not* be mutually exclusive, that is, it must be possible to put numbers in the intersection. For the extension activity, the intersecting Venn diagram on page 45 could be used.

**Developing Numeracy
Handling Data Year 3
© A & C Black**

Carroll or Venn labels

Teachers' sheet

- Cut out the labels and use them with Venn or Carroll diagrams.
  One-criterion Carroll – use two labels from the same row.
  One-criterion Venn – use one label.
  Two-criteria Carroll – use four labels from two rows.
  Two-criteria Venn (intersecting) – use two labels from different rows.
- Children can be asked to sort numbers up to 20, 50 or 100.

20 or less	More than 20
More than 15	15 or less
Odd numbers	Even numbers
Multiples of 2	Not multiples of 2
Multiples of 3	Not multiples of 3
Multiples of 4	Not multiples of 4
Multiples of 5	Not multiples of 5
Multiples of 10	Not multiples of 10
40 or less	More than 40
More than 25	25 or less

Teachers' note This sheet is a flexible resource for use with blank Venn and Carroll diagrams and the number cards on page 37. Copies of the blank Venn and Carroll diagrams on pages 45 and 46 could be enlarged on a photocopier for use in whole-class teaching. Encourage the children to compare the regions of the two types of diagrams.

Developing Numeracy
Handling Data Year 3
© A & C Black

Get it sorted!

You need a Carroll **or** Venn **diagram.**

• **Cut out the number cards.**

• **Sort them onto the diagram.**

1	2	3	4	5
6	7	8	9	10
11	12	13	14	15
16	17	18	19	20
21	22	23	24	25

Teachers' note Provide the children with an enlarged blank Venn or Carroll diagram from page 45 or 46. Give them appropriate labels from page 36 to put on the diagram or ask them to use other criteria such as 10 or less/more than 10; numbers with the digit 1, 2, 3, and so on; numbers made from straight lines/curved lines or both.

**Developing Numeracy
Handling Data Year 3
© A & C Black**

Sort it out!

• **Cut out the shape cards.**

1. Sort the shapes onto a Carroll diagram like this:

Triangles	Not triangles

2. Now sort the shapes onto a Carroll diagram like this:

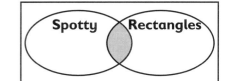

	Squares	Not squares
Stripes		
Not stripes		

3. Sort the shapes onto a Venn diagram like this:

Which cards are in the shaded section?

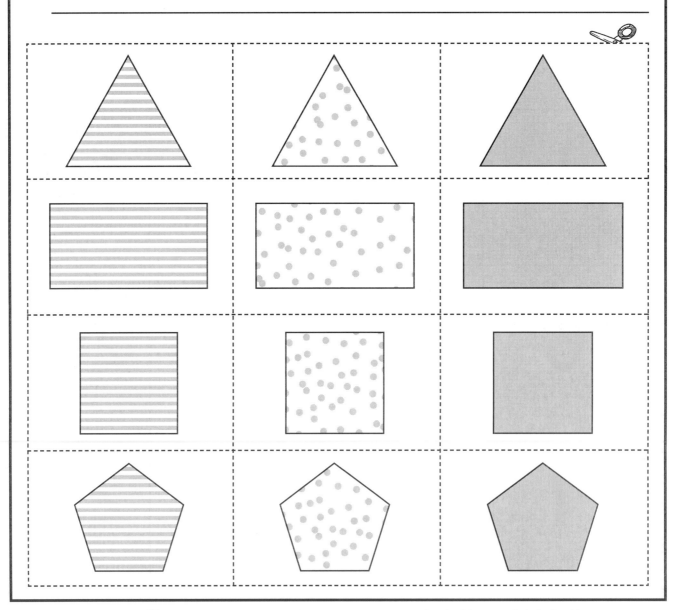

Teachers' note Provide enlarged blank Venn and Carroll diagrams from pages 45 and 46 for this activity, or let the children draw their own diagrams. Discuss the fact that a rectangle is a shape with four sides and four right angles, and that a square is a type of rectangle. The children could draw their own 2-D shapes on cards to add to their diagrams.

Developing Numeracy
Handling Data Year 3
© A & C Black

It's a marathon

Marathon runners wear numbers. Here are some
runners' numbers and the positions they came in a race.

Runner number	Position		Runner number	Position
36	1st		27	6th
16	2nd		21	7th
42	3rd		33	8th
22	4th		15	9th
12	5th		47	10th

- **Write the runners' numbers on the Carroll diagram.**

	Runner number 26 or higher	Runner number 25 or lower
5th position or better		
Lower than 5th position (6th, 7th, 8th, 9th or 10th)		

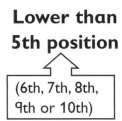

- **Look at the runners shown on your diagram.**

1. How many had numbers higher than 25? _____

2. How many had numbers that were 25 or lower? _____

3. How many in the top five had numbers higher than 25? _____

Teachers' note The children could also sort the information on this sheet using other criteria such as 'Even numbers' and 'Not even numbers'. They could then discuss whether they think those with even numbers were more likely to do well in the race (explain that there is no reason why this should be the case).

**Developing Numeracy
Handling Data Year 3
© A & C Black**

Legs and eyes

- ## Look carefully at the cards.

  1. Draw a bar chart to show the number of things with 2, 3, 4, 5 or 6 legs.

  2. Draw a bar chart to show the number of things with 0, 1, 2, 3 or 4 eyes.

- ## Now cut out the cards.

  3. Sort all the cards onto a Carroll diagram labelled **2 eyes/Not 2 eyes** and **4 legs/Not 4 legs**.

  4. Shuffle the cards. Sort them onto a Venn diagram with the rings labelled **Fewer than 2 eyes** and **More than 4 legs**.

  Which cards are in the middle section? _____

Teachers' note Ask the children to label the intervals on the bar charts in ones or twos. They could be given blank charts and diagrams from pages 44 to 46 (use the two-criteria intersecting Venn diagram on page 45 and the two-criteria Carroll diagram on page 46).

**Developing Numeracy
Handling Data Year 3
© A & C Black**

Data project: planning

People in our group

- **Read the list of topics.**

- **Decide together which topic to choose, or make up a topic of your own.**

✎ What is the most common kind of litter around our school?

✎ How do the contents of our group's pencil cases differ?

✎ What types of pet do children in our class own?

✎ How many pieces of maths equipment are there in the classroom that are plastic and for measuring?

Topic we have chosen

How we are going to find out the information (who will do what)

How we are going to record the information

What type of chart we might draw (choose from pictogram, bar chart, Venn diagram or Carroll diagram)

Teachers' note Use this with pages 42 and 43. Discuss this planning sheet with the whole class before organising the children into groups. Ensure that the children understand what is required, and suggest different ways in which they could work, distribute responsibility within the group, and record and present the information. Pages 44 to 46 could be used to help the children with this project.

**Developing Numeracy
Handling Data Year 3
© A & C Black**

Data project: collecting

People in our group

Our topic

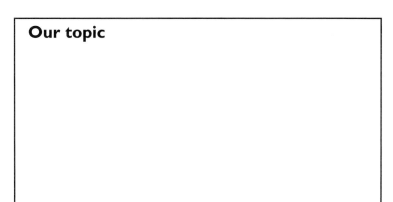

• **Use this table to help you collect your data.**

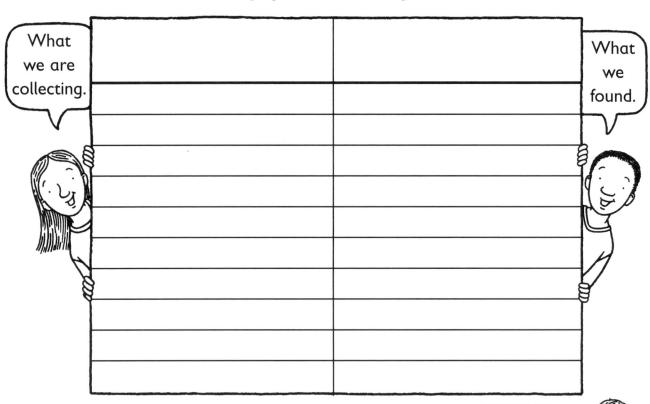

What we are collecting.

What we found.

• **Now you are going to draw a chart to show this information. Think carefully about how you will organise this.**

How will you label your chart?

  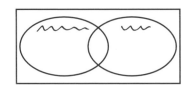 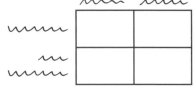

• **Talk to your teacher before you begin.**

Teachers' note Use this with pages 41 and 43. Encourage each child to draw their own chart. Information could be presented in various ways, for example, if exploring the contents of pencil cases, the horizontal axis could show the number of items and the vertical axis the number of people, or the horizontal axis could show each person's name with the number of items plotted up the side.

Developing Numeracy Handling Data Year 3 © A & C Black

Data project: interpreting

• **Look at these words.**

Most	How many...?
Most popular	How many more...?
Most common	How many fewer...?
	How many are... and...?
Least	...the same number as...
Least popular	...half as many as...
Least common	...twice as many as...

People in our group

• **Write statements about your chart using the words.**
  Try to write different ones from the rest of your group.

Teachers' note Use this with pages 41 and 42. The statements could be cut out and mounted on the wall next to the charts. Each group could plan a presentation to the rest of the class to share their information and show their charts. Discuss the information and ask specific questions, for example, *Seven people had the same thing... what was it?* or *Seven pieces of which type of litter were found?*

Developing Numeracy Handling Data Year 3 © A & C Black

Blank bar chart

A bar chart to show _____
_____

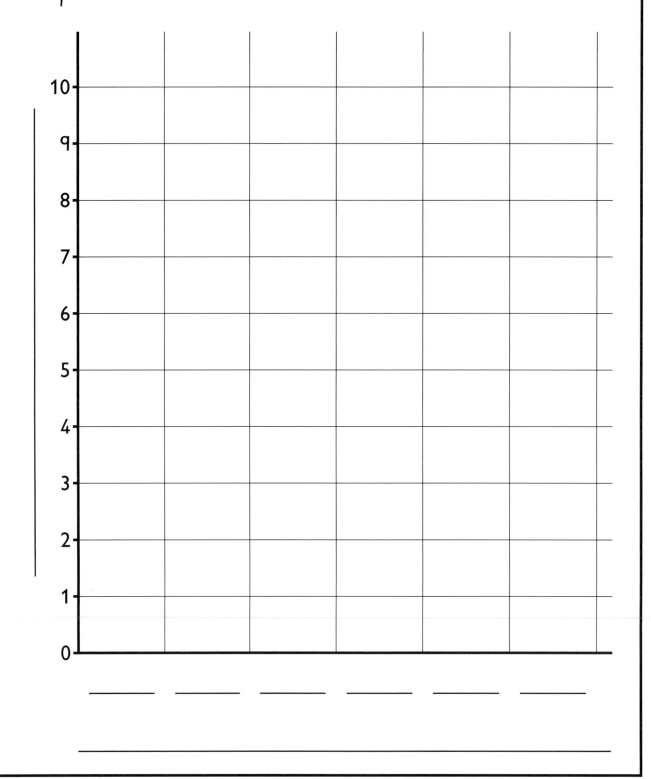

Teachers' note This sheet provides a flexible resource. It can be enlarged on a photocopier. Remind the children of the importance of labelling the axes and giving the chart a title. The odd numbers could be masked to allow children to work with intervals labelled in twos.

**Developing Numeracy
Handling Data Year 3
© A & C Black**

Blank Venn diagrams

One-criterion Venn

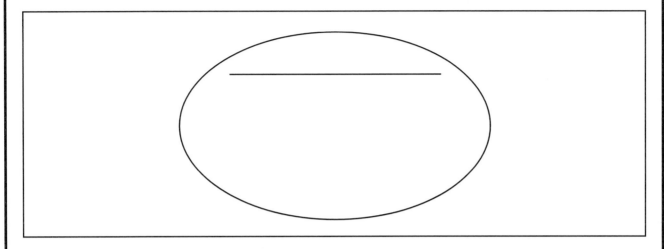

Two-criteria Venn (non-intersecting)

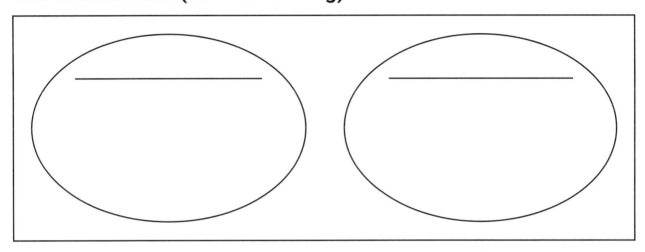

Two-criteria Venn (intersecting)

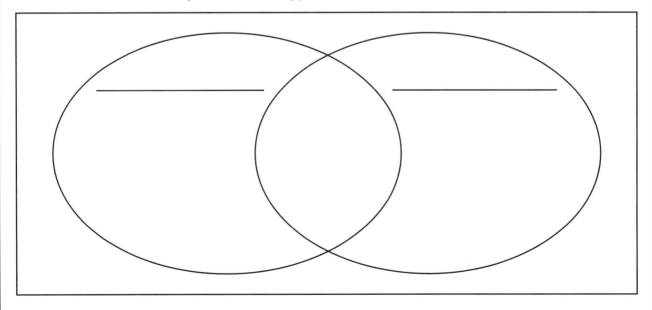

Teachers' note This sheet provides a flexible resource. It can be enlarged on a photocopier.

**Developing Numeracy
Handling Data Year 3
© A & C Black**

Blank Carroll diagrams

One-criterion Carroll

_____   _____

Two-criteria Carroll

_____   _____

_____

_____

Teachers' note This sheet provides a flexible resource. It can be enlarged on a photocopier.

**Developing Numeracy
Handling Data Year 3
© A & C Black**

p 6

Fruit	Number
bananas	6
pineapples	3
pears	5
apples	7
bunches of grapes	5
melons	1

1. Apples
2. Melons
3. Pineapples
4. 27
Now try this!
Melon, because the gorilla has eaten more melons.

p 8

In any order:
Aberdeen   8
Edinburgh   9
York   4
Manchester   10
Belfast   7
Liverpool   9
Norwich   7
Birmingham   10
Cardiff   7
London   6
Exeter   6
Canterbury   10

p 9

Engines with 1 carriage   2
Engines with 2 carriages   5
Engines with 3 carriages   4
Engines with 4 carriages   3

1. (a) 2   **(b)** 4   **(c)** 7   **(d)** 3
2. 2
3. 1
Now try this!
10

p 10

Monday   2
Tuesday   0
Wednesday 1
Thursday   1
Friday   1
Saturday   2
Sunday   3
Now try this!
£1

p 11

If the symbol represents 1 game:
1. 3
2. 0
3. Monday
4. Saturday
5. Sunday
6. (a) 6   **(b)** 11
7. She was not at school.
8. Wednesday and Friday
Now try this!
17

If the symbol represents 2 games:
1. 6
2. 0
3. Thursday
4. Monday
5. Sunday
6. (a) 12   **(b)** 22
7. She was not at school.
8. Wednesday and Friday

Now try this!
34

p 14
1. (a) 0   **(b)** 8   **(c)** 0   **(d)** 1
2. (a) Thursday   **(b)** Monday
3. (a) Saturday and Sunday
    (b) These are not school days.

p 15
1. Brown
2. Grey
3. (a) 8   **(b)** 1   **(c)** 3   **(d)** 11
4. 2
5. 5
6. 3
7. Discuss the children's answers.

p 16
Check statements are joined correctly.
Now try this!
True
True

p 20
1. (a) 3   **(b)** 6   **(c)** 5   **(d)** 5   **(e)** 4
2. Yes
3. No
4. 3
Now try this!
23

p 22
Bees 9   Butterflies 4   Horses 2   Cows 5   Rabbits 3

p 23
1. (a) 6   **(b)** 10
2. 5
3. 1
4. Tuesday and Wednesday
5. (a) 31   **(b)** 27   **(c)** 32

p 24
Missing coins: 1p, 5p, 50p, £2

p 25
1. 6
2. 5p
3. 9, or 11 if the £2 coins are included
4. 2p, 20p and £2
5. 13
6. 2
7. 8
8. 11
9. 19
10. 21p
11. £6.65
12. 35p

p 26

Number of people in each car	Number of cars
1	1
2	4
3	8
4	5
5	2

p27
1. (a) 8   **(b)** 5   **(c)** 2   **(d)** 1   **(e)** 7   **(f)** 5
2. 2
3. 20
4. 4
5. 63

p30
1. (a) 2   **(b)** 4   **(c)** 4   **(d)** 8
2. (a) 1   **(b)** 3
3. 1
4. 6
5. (a) 3   **(b)** 9
6. Sugar
7. 2

p31
1. (a) 8   **(b)** 16   **(c)** 16   **(d)** 32
2. 5
3. 40
4. 7
5. Bacon
6. 12
7. 3

p32
The ringed numbers are all multiples of 5.

p33
1. 6
2. 6
3. 9
4. 21

p35
1. 10
2. 14
3. (a) 6, 12, 18, 24, 30
   (b) 6 (and 1)
4. 7, 5, 17, 25, 13, 19, 29, 23, 1
5. Check the children's diagrams.

p38
1. Check sorting.
2. Check sorting.
3. Check sorting.
   Spotty rectangle and spotty square are in the shaded section.

p39

	Runner number 26 or higher	Runner number 25 or lower
5th position or better	36 42	16 22 12
Lower than 5th position (6th, 7th, 8th, 9th or 10th)	27 33 47	21 15

1. 5
2. 5
3. 2

p40
1. Check bar chart:
   6 things with 2 legs
   4 things with 3 legs
   7 things with 4 legs
   3 things with 5 legs
   0 things with 6 legs
2. Check bar chart:
   10 things with 0 eyes
   1 thing with 1 eye
   8 things with 2 eyes
   0 things with 3 eyes
   1 thing with 4 eyes
3. Check sorting.
4. Check sorting.
   Chairs are in the middle section.